Published in 2011 by Prion
An imprint of the Carlton Publishing Group
20 Mortimer Street
London W1T 3JW

10 9 8 7 6 5 4 3 2 1

A CIP catalogue record for this book is available from the British Library.

ISBN 978-1-85375-809-6

Printed and bound by CPI Mackays, Chatham ME5 8TD

Illustrations: Anna Stiles

The material in this book was previously published in *Things a Father Should Know*

SUPER DAD

JOKES, FUN AND ADVICE
FOR EVERY FAMILY'S FAVOURITE HERO

JIM MALONEY

PRION

CONTENTS

CONTENTS

INTRODUCTION

So how does it feel to be the World's Greatest Dad? What do you mean 'Better ask someone else?' To your child or children you are the World's Greatest Dad, however woefully you might think you do the job.

You might not be the best football player, the fittest dad in the park when it comes to running around or one of those dads who seems to be able to buy his kids whatever they want. Let's face it, nobody is perfect, but your kids wouldn't have you any other way. One little boy, when his father embarked on a post-Christmas exercise regime to lose a few pounds, said to his mother, 'Daddies aren't really meant to be skinny, are they?' His dad never had been, so as far as he was concerned, that's the way dads were meant to be.

Every father's relationship with his child is unique and every child, boy or girl, looks upon their dad in a different way.

Whatever the differences, however, to your child, you are the greatest, but living up to their expectations is a real challenge. It's a challenge made easier to tackle with a healthy dose of good humour and the benefit of the experiences of others.

Things a Father Should Know is not an instruction manual, but a collection of warm, delightful and amusing tales from dads in the know, including some 'Dad's Jokes' – because every dad is supposed to keep a sense of humour, even when work, the family, the bank manager and the tax man are all hounding him!

Put your feet up and delve into *Things a Father Should Know*, even if it's only to take some comfort from the fact that other dads have it just as tough as you do!

If the new father feels
bewildered and even defeated,
let him take comfort from the fact
that whatever he does in any fathering
situation has a fifty per cent chance
of being right.

Bill Cosby

PREPARING FOR FATHERHOOD

You've read the baby books, been to the pre-natal classes and already bonded with the bulge in your wife's tummy. You're fully prepared, primed and ready for fatherhood. Dear friend....
Whatever preparation you make it will be totally inadequate for the reality. So don't work out for fatherhood like a millipede on a running-machine. Here's all you need to know.

READ BEFORE FATHERHOOD

1) Don't worry, your dad didn't know what he was doing, either.

2) Just make it up as you go along.

3) Relax. Some boys do like to dress up and play with dolls. They will probably grow out of it. And if they don't well, hey-ho.

4) Your house will never be tidy again.

5) There's never enough food in the house.

6) Never disclose to other parents that you have found a good baby-sitter.

7) Let them make their own mistakes. It's the best way to learn.

8) Dropping food on the floor is a new and delightful skill to a one-year-old, not a deliberate attempt to annoy you.

9) Daughters learn how to flirt alarmingly quickly.

10) Even when you know you are big manipulated you will be powerless to stop it.

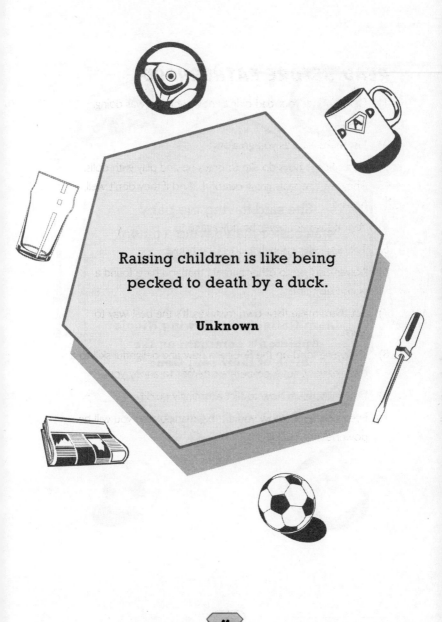

Raising children is like being
pecked to death by a duck.

Unknown

She said having the baby
was easier than having a tattoo.
I really don't know what sort of
tattoo parlours she's been to!

**Liam Gallagher following Nicole
Appleton's comment on the
birth of their son, Gene.**

TO BE OR NOT TO BE

That is the question. We are talking about whether or not to be present at the birth, of course. While some dads wouldn't dream of being anywhere else, others would rather be anywhere else. If you fall into the latter category then you'll find it hard to come up with a decent excuse for not being there. After all, many fathers say that seeing their child born was the most amazing experience they have ever had. So why, your other half might ask, wouldn't you want to experience it yourself?

The usual excuses of "I can't take time off work," or "I'm not feeling very well," don't really cut it. Chef Gordon Ramsay doesn't mince his words, though. He was upfront with his wife, Tana, about his reason not to be there.

"We have a very active sex life and we both sat down and contemplated over a bottle of wine that it wasn't good for our sexual relationship for me to be at childbirth," he said. "I told her I'd feel squeamish seeing that level of mess. It's like sending 25 vegans into a kitchen with meat in the blender."

HEARING IS BELIEVING

Tom never fancied watching his wife give birth and, fortunately for him, he managed to avoid it with both of their children.

"When our first child was born, my wife Sadie was suddenly rushed off to have an emergency caesarean after oxygen stopped getting through to the baby," he recalls. "I was just left sitting in the hospital, shell-shocked, wondering whether I would ever see her again.

"A few years after the birth of our daughter, Sadie fell pregnant again and, because of the complications first time round, elected to have a caesarean. This is not really a spectator sport – thank goodness – and so I sat behind her head as the medics got to grips with things down the business end behind a conveniently placed screen.

"I couldn't see anything but the alarming sucking and slurping noises sounded like something out of the film *Alien*. My worries increased when one of the nurses remarked, 'This baby is enormous!' I thought to myself, 'What on earth have we got here?' But it turned out to be just a reasonably-sized baby boy, weighing in at 8lb 12oz."

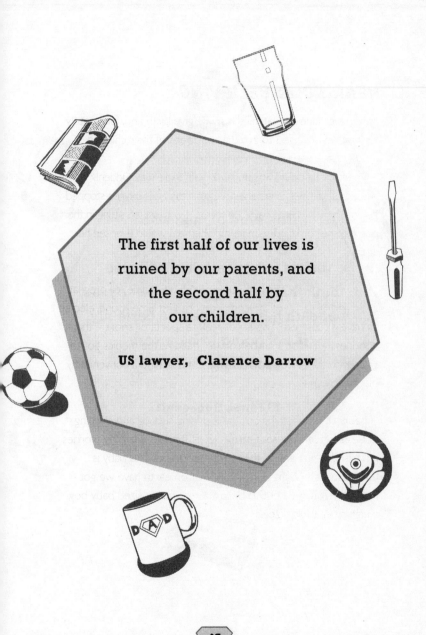

The first half of our lives is ruined by our parents, and the second half by our children.

US lawyer, Clarence Darrow

The kind of man who
thinks that helping with the
dishes is beneath him will also
think that helping with the baby is
beneath him, and then he certainly
is not going to be a very
successful father.

Eleanor Roosevelt

PREGNANT DADS

Fathers experience the symptoms of pregnancy too, you know. Well… some of them. Morning sickness, headache, weight gain, doesn't necessarily mean that you have been on an all-night bender. One study showed that 90 per cent of men experience at least one pregnancy-related symptom, sometimes severe enough to prompt an expectant father to seek medical help!

SLEEPING LIKE A BABY

When US senator John McCain was asked by chat show host Jay Leno about how he was coping after his defeat in the US presidential election, he replied: "I've been sleeping like a baby – sleep two hours, wake up and cry, sleep two hours, wake up and cry."

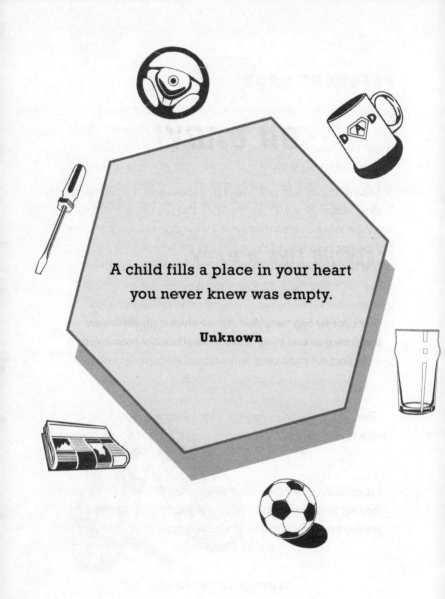

A child fills a place in your heart
you never knew was empty.

Unknown

OH BABY!

Leaving hospital with your wife and newborn baby is daunting. For some reason the nurses seem to think that you are now equipped to cope. What an absurd notion! You know next to nothing. And one of the first indications of this is trying to get baby into the baby seat and strapped into the car. You have never had to do this before… and it shows.

It's not for beginners. Working out which strap goes where and fiddling around trying to adjust lengths whilst baby is getting fractious and waiting wife irritated, will be a demand on your patience.

Then, just as you finally have straps in place and buckles aligned ready to clunk together, they slip out of your fingers and you have to start again.

It is, no doubt, a joke that nurses play on new fathers. Knowing that they will be all fingers and thumbs trying to take baby home, they sneakily peep at you from a window and giggle at your clumsiness and increasing anger.

It's even funnier if it's raining.

YOU MEAN, I HAVE TO LOOK AFTER IT?

Once you have the baby home in your house, life will never be the same again. You will be like an unpaid servant pandering to this tiny emperor's demands. After a while you will be so immersed in your role that you will look back in amazement at the pre-baby days when you had so much freedom. Time was your own, then. Why the heck didn't you make the most of it?

Yes, it will be hectic at times and stressful but that gurgling, smiling face, dribbling mouth and look of utter contentment… will have you thinking of Pete, in the pub on a Saturday night (or any other night, come to that). Why aren't you there? Because you have the responsibility of being a father. Any escape to the pub must now be viewed as a luxury and one for which your wife will make you pay heavily. Just because she says she doesn't mind you going for a quick drink with the boys, doesn't mean that she doesn't mind. And when you come back later than arranged and a little the worse for wear and she asks if you had a good night, don't assume that she is the slightest bit interested in your reply.

You are now in her debt. Prepare for some 'extra' father duties.

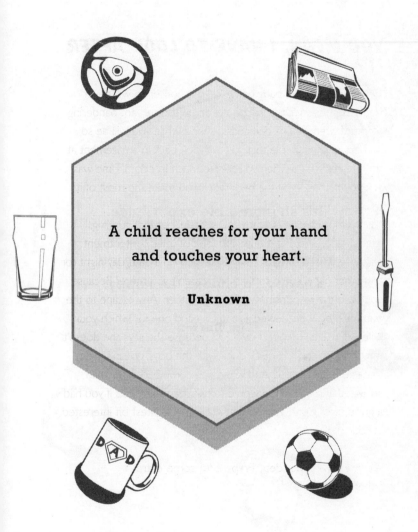

A child reaches for your hand
and touches your heart.

Unknown

It's an incredible experience. If I had a choice about going to a meeting at a studio or changing a nappy, I'd choose the nappy.

Tim Burton

NAPPY DAYS

The days when mum always changed the baby's nappy are long gone. You will be expected to do it, so face up to it. The good news is that it's not as bad as you think. Even so, it is always a shock the first time that you remove your son's nappy and he is lying naked on his back and starts to pee over the top of his head! Quite impressive, too.

But with disposable nappies, wet wipes and scented nappy sacks, changing a nappy is really not such a big deal. And if you can deposit the dirty nappy in your neighbour's bin instead of your own, then it's a bonus.

WHAT'S THAT SMELL?

Colin was enjoying his holiday in Tuscany with his wife, Kirsty, their toddler, Edward, and their best friends, Graham and Hayley. Carrying Edward on his shoulders, he was enjoying the sights, but only one thing was disturbing him. What was that horrible smell? Of course, it must be Edward's nappy. No problem. He would change it. With a fresh nappy on, Edward looked happy and content. Unfortunately, the same couldn't be said for Colin because it wasn't long before he could smell it again. Another nappy change. Hmm… seems pretty clean.

As the day continued, Colin made several nappy checks and tried to avoid the smell. Eventually he could take no more and asked, "Has anyone else noticed that horrid smell? It's been following me around all day!"

His wife and friends looked sheepish before Kirsty confessed, "Well, actually you've had baby poo down the back of your shirt all day. We thought it best not to tell you."

I remember so clearly us going into hospital so Victoria could have Brooklyn. I was eating a Lion Bar at the time.

David Beckham

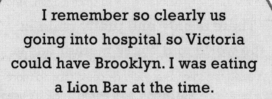

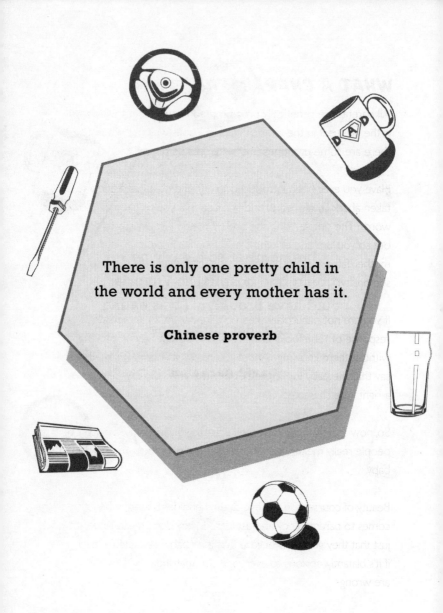

There is only one pretty child in the world and every mother has it.

Chinese proverb

WHAT A CHARACTER!

All parents are genetically programmed to think that their baby is the prettiest in the world. Which is just as well, really, because there are some ugly ones out there, let's be honest.

Have you ever been introduced to a friend's baby and been so taken aback by it's red, prune-like face that you've been lost for words? The simple, "Isn't she pretty?" cliché just refuses to come out so you 'um and er' whilst searching for inspiration as the mother/father's smile begins to fade until you finally blurt, "Isn't she pretty?"

If you are not particularly keen on the parent an immediate response of, "She looks just like you," is a great way of insulting without them knowing. And if you really can't bring yourself to say that the baby looks pretty, then just smile and say, "She looks a right little character."

So, now that you can read the sub-text, you will know what people really mean when they comment on your own gorgeous baby.

Beauty, of course, is in the eye of the beholder. But not when it comes to parents. They are just biased. They don't mean to be, it's just that they genuinely believe that their baby is beautiful – even if it's blatantly obvious to everyone else that they are wrong.

Interestingly, many parents look back at photographs of their babies, once they are older, and are startled to realise that they weren't as pretty as they imagined. But, by then, they have the prettiest toddler in the world.

DAD APPEAL

It's a strange thing, but when women see a father carrying his baby, on his own, then they go all gooey. Ahh! You won't be prepared for this and initially you will be wondering why women are smiling at you. It never happened before, after all. But if you think they are flirting with you, then you've totally misread what's going.

They just think you are a sweet and loving father. They don't know, of course, that you can't wait to get home and dump the baby on your wife. But if you come over all smiley and fatherly-like, then you will attract even more female attention. It's amazing.

Ironic, isn't it? All these years when you have been 'unbothered' by female attention, now you have it in spade-loads but only because they think of you as a 'safe' father. Oh, well. You might as well make the most of what you can get.

GOING OUT CHECKLIST

Baby	Car seat
Nappies	Nappy sacks
Wipes	Baby cream
Change of clothes	Milk
Bottles	Food
Bib	Rattle
Fluffy toy	Travel cot
Pram	Water-proof cover
Sun shade	Blanket

Sometimes it's easier just to stay at home!

Blokes can watch but can't know what it feels like to have a baby. One woman I spoke to said a caesarean feels like someone doing the washing up in your stomach.

Tony Parsons

THREE TIMES UNLUCKY?

Simon and his wife, Fiona, decided not to have any more babies after Simon lost his job following the birth of both of his children.

"On both occasions I was on paternity leave when I heard the news," he said. "The first time I was at home with my baby daughter when I had a phone call from the office saying that the magazine I worked on had 'folded' and that I was being made redundant.

"I got another job and two years later my wife gave birth to a boy. I visited my wife and son in hospital and was feeling all warm and cosy inside as I got into the car to return home. I was still in the hospital car park when I received a call on my mobile from my office saying that they hoped the baby was well etc., before adding that I had been made redundant. No need to come in after paternity leave was through. They would kindly pack up my belongings and send them on.

"We decided not to have another baby after that. I also decided never to have another full-time employer. I have been self-employed ever since and have, so far, avoided being sacked!"

I DIDN'T HEAR A THING

Selective hearing is a wonderful thing. Baby crying? What baby crying? Oh, that baby crying. I didn't hear it.

Tucked up in bed, warm and cosy, a picture of innocence… no, not the baby, you. Suddenly you are aware of a distant crying that gets louder and louder as it enters your sub-conscience.

Oh, no! It's the baby! You have never felt so snug and the thought of getting up and dealing with your baby is enough to have you rolling back onto your side and dropping off to sleep again. If it wasn't for the noise.

Wait! There's two of us here. Isn't it my wife's turn to get up and see to the baby? After all, she is the mother. And there is an undeniable bond between mother and baby that you would be loathe to come between. Surely she's heard the baby crying? Yes! She's stirring. Stay still now. Maybe ease into some heavy breathing and a little snore so she will think you are asleep.

Meanwhile, the crying is getting louder and angrier. Your wife has stopped moving and so have you. It's stalemate. You both know, by now, that no one could actually sleep through the din.

I think God made babies cute
so we don't eat them.

Robin Williams

You're kidding each other. It's a game of wills. Who will break first?
As you lie there, frightened to stir, you curse the fact that you
can change a nappy as well as she can. But it's worse than that.
You have drawn the short straw because the baby isn't breast fed
which means that you can feed it just as well, too!

THERE'S A DIG IN YOUR RIBS.

"The baby's crying," murmurs the wife, as if she has just woken
up and noticed. Some chance!

"Who? What? Where?" you reply – a masterclass of method
acting.

"Baby. Crying," says wife.

"Uh? Baby? Oh. Right . . . Isn't it *your* turn?"

"No! I think you'll find it's *your* turn."

From here on you are in a 'no win situation.' If you insist that it is
your wife's turn and force her to deal with it, then you will feel so
guilty that it will almost ruin your sleep. Almost. And if you decide
to do the manly thing and get up and deal with it yourself, then
you will feel tired, angry and, probably cold.

The choice is yours.

34

MOMENT TO SAVOUR

"Of all the sensations of joy and release that nature in her kindness has bestowed on the human race, there is little or nothing to beat the moment when you get rid of the baby's car seat," according to London Mayor Boris Johnson. "It beats getting off a long haul flight. It beats taking off a pair of ill-fitting ski boots after a hard day on the slopes. It verges, frankly, on the orgasmic."

A WEE CHANGE

Rod changed baby Ava's nappy on their freshly-laundered duvet and told his wife, Julia, not to be so uptight when she suggested that he use the changing mat.

"When he looked and realised our duvet was covered in wee, I'm pretty sure he made a mental note never to do it again!" said Julia.

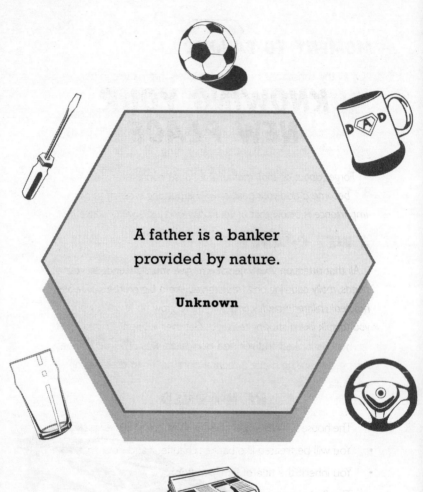

A father is a banker
provided by nature.

Unknown

KNOWING YOUR NEW PLACE

Forget about all that 'man of the house' nonsense. Once you become a dad your position in the pecking order of family importance is below that of your baby and just slightly above that of the family pet (if you're lucky).

All that attention your wife used to give you, pandering to your needs, molly coddling and treating you like a big child. It's over. She has real children now. It's time for you to grow up. It won't work for you to sulk like a stroppy teenager. Get over it, get helping and get a thick skin. You'll need it.

BE WARNED

- The house will never again be tidy. Well, not until they leave.

- You will be treated like banker, chauffeur and door-mat.

- You inherit the title of family buffoon.

- The first sarcastic comment from your child will leave you speechless.

- When your child tells you off you will feel like a naughty schoolboy.

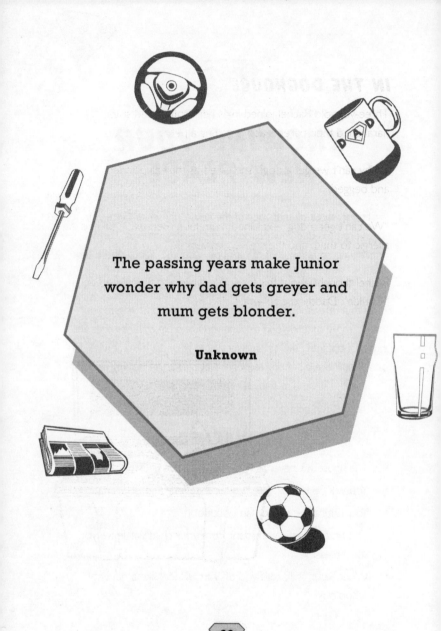

The passing years make Junior
wonder why dad gets greyer and
mum gets blonder.

Unknown

IN THE DOGHOUSE

Three-year-old Rachel joined in as her brother and sister harangued their parents about getting a pet.

"Why can't we get a dog?" she asked, as they all pleaded and begged.

"We can't get a dog," explained mum Julie. "Because Daddy is allergic to them and they make him very ill."

Rachel thought about this for a little while and then piped up: "Couldn't Daddy just go away?"

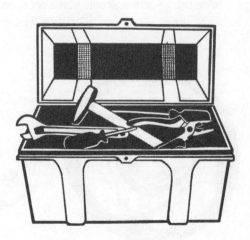

KEEP THAT MAN OUT!

Hard-working Jim couldn't wait to get back home to see his young daughter, Georgia, when he left the office each evening. The smile on her face and warm cuddle quickly dissolved the stresses of the day. But then things started to change. Or rather, Georgia did.

At the age of three, having spent hours at home just with mum, she began to resent dad coming home. The resentment gradually turned to horror with her screaming and in floods of tears whenever she heard dad turn the key in the lock. She even tried to hold the door closed! This unsettling phase went on for a few weeks before, much to dad's relief, she started giving him a warm welcome home once more.

Children divide into two types, the ones who come into your bed and lie still, and the ones that wriggle. Leo is a wriggler. So once he gets in, you find a foot in your ear.

Former PM Tony Blair on his youngest son.

A father carries pictures
where his money used to be.

Unknown

10 REASONS TO MAKE YOURSELF SCARCE

1) Your daughter has invited her friends for a sleepover.

2) Your wife is having a 'mums get-together' in the house.

3) The kids are restless and you hear the word 'park' mentioned.

4) You hear your wife saying, "Ask daddy to do it."

5) It's the kids' bath time.

6) You hear that plastic cascade of Lego bricks being tipped out of the box.

7) You catch a faint whiff of full nappy.

8) A row erupts upstairs between mother and offspring.

9) You hear the words "We'll have to go shopping and get you a new one."

10) Granny is on her way over.

EARLY EXPERIMENT

While campaigning for the New Jersey governorship in 1940, Charles Edison was careful to distance himself from his famous inventor father, Thomas. "I would not have anyone believe I am trading on the name Edison," he said, before adding, "I would rather have you know me merely as the result of one of my father's earlier experiments."

A DOG'S LIFE

Overheard at an airport was a mother talking to her young son. "Now remember," she said. "Run to Dad first, then the dog."

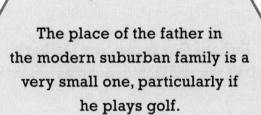

The place of the father in the modern suburban family is a very small one, particularly if he plays golf.

Bertrand Russell

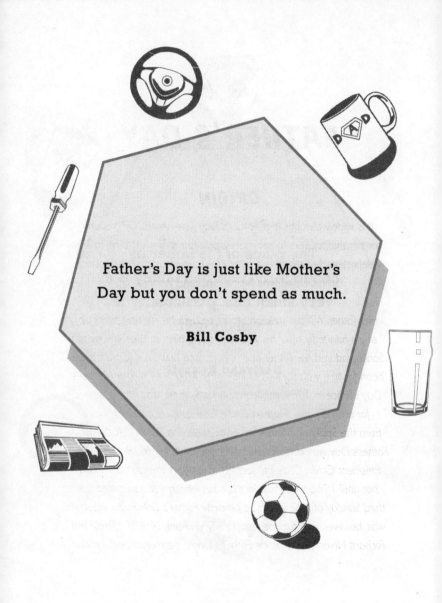

Father's Day is just like Mother's
Day but you don't spend as much.

Bill Cosby

FATHER'S DAY

ORIGIN

It is widely thought that Father's Day was created by greeting card manufacturers to sell more cards. But that's just a myth. The celebration developed in America from an idea by Sonora Louise Smart Dodd, who lived in Spokane, Washington.

Her father, William Jackson Smart, brought his six daughters up single-handedly after his wife died giving birth to their youngest. Sonora adored her father and appreciated how hard it must have been for him with six kids to look after. After attending a Mother's Day service in 1909, she wondered why there was no equivalent for dads. So she started gaining local support and, with help from the Spokane Ministerial Association and the YMCA, the first Father's Day was celebrated in Spokane on June 19, 1910. In 1924, President Calvin Coolidge decided to support the idea, but it was not until 1966 that President Lyndon Johnson declared that the third Sunday of June would be officially Father's Day in the US. This was, however, only for one year. Finally, on April 24, 1972, President Richard Nixon finally made Father's Day a permanent celebration.

AROUND THE WORLD

Many other countries, such as Britain and Canada also celebrate Father's Day on the third Sunday of June. In Australia and New Zealand it's on the first Sunday of September whilst for Spain and Belgium it falls on 19 March. Sweden celebrates Father's Day every second Sunday in November.

WORST FATHER'S DAY GIFTS (AND WHAT THEY MEAN)

- Tie – Depressingly, it is the most common Father's Day gift. It's also one of the most boring things a dad can receive. If you wear a tie for work it will just remind you of the office. And if you don't wear one for work then you won't be wearing it much, anyway.

- Nose hair clippers – Staggeringly awful. Just what do your kids think of you?

- Mug saying – 'World's Best Dad.' Yes, it's a nice sentiment but millions of these trashy things are being given out all over the world.

- Multi coloured jumper – It just looks like 'interference' on the TV.

- Socks – Yawn!

A child is a curly, dimpled lunatic.

Ralph Waldo Emerson

If I turn into my parents, I'll either be an alcoholic blonde chasing 21-year-old boys, or I'll wind up like my mother.

Chandler Bing, Friends

- Soap on a rope – What a ropey concept.

- Screwdriver – So dads are just for DIY?

- Slippers – It's Father's Day, not Granddad's Day!

A survey in Australia revealed that the worst presents Aussie dads have received were a book on financial management, a vacuum cleaner, an IOU, nose hair clippers and a tub of putty. (a tub of *putty*??) Another dad received chocolate-covered peanuts, despite being allergic to nuts.

WASH TIME

Trying to be helpful proved to be a disaster for one dad when he put a load of family clothes into the washing machine.

"When I took the clothes out, I discovered, to my dismay, that I had also washed the watch my wife had given me while we were dating," he said.

"She wasn't happy and frostily remarked, 'Don't expect me to replace it.' By the time Father's Day rolled around, however, she had relented and gave me a beautiful new watch.

"Attached was a note with this stipulation: 'DRY-CLEAN ONLY!'"

TOP 10 SONGS FOR DADS

Papa Don't Preach – Madonna

Don't Cry Daddy – Elvis Presley

Dance With My Father – Luther Vandross

The Living Years – Mike and the Mechanics

My Father's Eyes – Eric Clapton

Papa Was a Rolling Stone - Temptations

Father And Son – Cat Stevens

Father and Daughter - Paul Simon

Just The Two Of Us - Will Smith

I Don't Want To Miss A Thing – Aerosmith

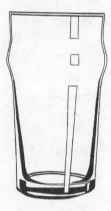

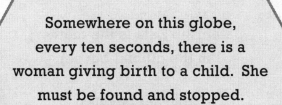

Somewhere on this globe,
every ten seconds, there is a
woman giving birth to a child. She
must be found and stopped.

Sam Levenson

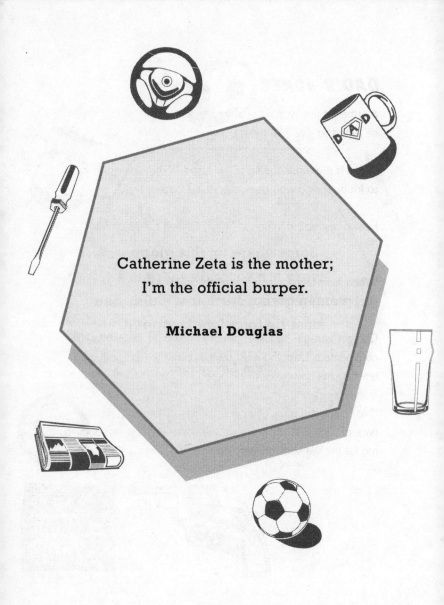

Catherine Zeta is the mother;
I'm the official burper.

Michael Douglas

DAD'S JOKES

A father of five won a toy at a raffle and, calling his kids together, he aimed to give it to the most worthy.

"Who is the most obedient?" he asked. "Who never talks back to Mother? And who does everything Mother says?"

Five voices replied in unison. "Okay, Daddy! You get the toy."

When their teenage son passed his driving test, the family celebrated by getting in the car as he drove them around.

Dad got into the back seat, directly behind the driver. His son commented: "Dad, you must be fed up of the front seat after teaching me how to drive all these days. Right?"

"No," came the reply. "I'm going to sit back here and kick the back of your seat while you drive, just like you've been doing to me for the last sixteen years!"

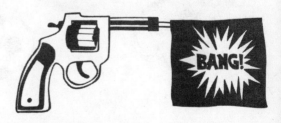

My son isn't the slightest bit impressed when he sees me on TV. He'd much rather watch SpongeBob SquarePants and I don't blame him.

Actor Todd Carty

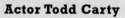

HOW TO IMPRESS
YOUR KIDS

If you have a natural talent for something – football, art, glass-blowing – then it's easy to impress your kids. Right? Wrong! The truth is, kids get bored very quickly and are soon totally unimpressed by whatever skill you have. So you need to be continually inventive. But the trick is not to try too hard. After all, you don't want to raise their expectations. The more 'spontaneous' it appears, the more effect it will have. But what impresses them the most in the long-run is simply to play with them.

Younger kids are much easier to impress than older. When they are babies just the simple act of you throwing a ball into the air and catching it leaves them gurgling with delight. Sadly, after such a good start, it's downhill from here on. The only thing you can do is attempt to slow down the decline.

When I was a boy of 14, my father was so ignorant I could hardly stand to have the old man around. But when I got to be 21, I was astonished at how much the old man had learned in seven years.

Mark Twain

THE WONDER YEARS

Below is a list of the marking posts on the slippery slope from awe to pity…

Baby: Goo goo gah gah!!

3 years: Wow! How did you do that?

6 years: I know how to do that.

9 years: Oh, Dad!

12 years: You don't do it like that!

14 years: Whatever.

18 years: (silent, pitying look)

ALL AT SEA

Having re-watched *Jaws* recently, Barry came over all 'Quint-like' when he went on holiday to Cornwall and promptly booked a fishing trip on a boat with his son.

Wearing the bright yellow weatherproof clothing he had bought, he certainly stood out from the small crowd as they boarded the boat. He would be bringing home the dinner tonight, he had informed his wife. Fresh fish for all.

Looking out to sea with a steely eye, Barry felt every inch the rugged fisherman. As the boat headed out, he put a fatherly hand on his son's shoulder and asked him if he was okay. "Yeah, great!" young Michael replied. Barry was in his element.

"This is great father-son bonding," he thought. But when the captain turned off the boat's engine, the swaying movement began to make Barry feel distinctly sick.

"Are we going to do some fishing now, Dad?" Michael asked. By way of answer, Barry was promptly sick over the side. Unfortunately, that was just where the group was about to fish from and there were some audible expressions of disgust amongst one or two sympathetic remarks.

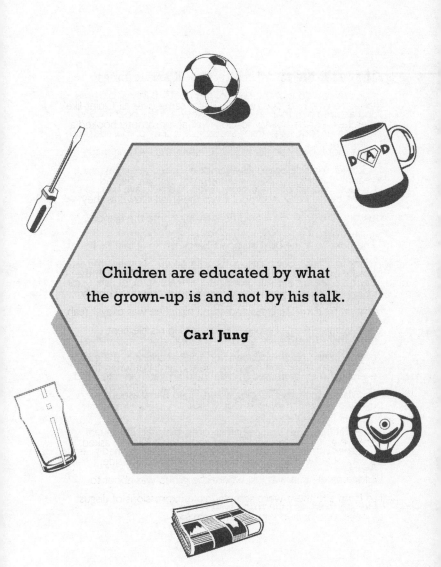

Children are educated by what
the grown-up is and not by his talk.

Carl Jung

The captain had a word in Barry's ear: "If you are going to be sick, can you do it at the back of the boat?" Barry apologised and assured him that he was okay now. As the boat moved to another spot, away from the sick slick, they prepared to fish once more. Barry began to join in when the swaying made him sick over the side again. As everyone looked at him aghast, the boat moved off once more. Even Michael gave his dad a withering look.

The next time the boat stopped, Barry felt so ill that he had to retire to a bunk down below for a lie down. He spent the entire day here feeling awful. It didn't help when a stack of fishing rods fell on top of him from a shelf above.

Poor Barry thought the day would never end. He remained on the bunk until the boat arrived back at shore in the early evening. An embarrassed Michael held his 'catch' in one hand and dad in the other, leading green-faced Barry ashore.

They did have fish that night. The ones that Michael caught, together with some that a pitying fellow passenger had given to Barry.

He later sold his fisherman's waterproofs.

10 EASY WAYS TO IMPRESS YOUR KIDS

1. Show them your old superhero comic collection.

2. Draw something half-way decent.

3. Make a 'balloon animal.'

4. Do a magic trick.

5. Juggle.

6. Give them an unexpected treat.

7. Make them a tree house.

8. Decorate their room.

9. Win them a toy at the fair.

10. Play with them.

If all the world thought and
acted like children, we'd never
have any trouble. The only pity is,
even kids have to grow up.

Walt Disney

THE FUN OF THE FAIR

You've taken the kids along to the fair and they've frittered away your 'agreed' allowance of money in less than five minutes. Now the pressure is on. Those cheap and nasty 'cuddly' toys may look like they have been made by an ogre in the dark but your kids will want one, anyway. Of course, you'll never win one of the big, well-made ones. That's not because you haven't got what it takes. It's simply that no one ever wins them. They are un-winnable.

After several pleads of, "Dad! Dad! Win me a cuddly toy!" it's time to step up to the mark. You've always secretly fancied your chances as a cowboy, so the rifle range calls. The target may be ducks, stacked cans or enemy soldiers. It doesn't matter. The sights on these rifles are purely ornamental and of no practical use whatsoever. Blam! Blam! Blam! "Unlucky! Wanna try again?"

"Yeah! Go on, Dad!" Blam! Blam! Blam! "I tell you what, kids. Lets try ringing the bell with the hammer."

Minutes later... having embarrassed yourself by getting nowhere near the bell, the sense of disappoint felt by you, your kids, wife and spectators, is unbearable. Your face is red with shame as you quickly move away. Where to? It doesn't matter. Anywhere is better.

So, it's down to that old favourite – the coconut shy. Now, no one actually wants a coconut. No one likes them. They can only be opened by smashing them to smithereens and the small amount of juice inside – the nice bit – is lost. But that's not the point. It's about winning one.

You can do this. All is not lost. Here's the opportunity to show that you are not a wuss who can't even win an argument. It may not be a cuddly toy, but it no longer matters. As long as you win *something!*

As you hurl ball after ball at nothing, you decide that less power and more aim is the answer. Another go then. And another one. Bullseye! Whacked it right in the middle! But wait… it has hardly budged! If anything, it has sunk even lower into the cup! The stall holder shrugs in a fake apologetic sort of way. You pay for another go. Look at those balls fly through the air! Okay, one more go. Got it! But it just wobbles. Last go. You're getting desperate now. The wife is calling you away. Even the kids are bored. But it's no longer about them. This is between man and coconut.

Eventually, your wife forcibly drags you off. You have spent a small fortune and come away empty handed. The kids are no longer bothered. But the shame will last a lot longer than that rip-off fairground visit!

SALAD DAYS

Back in the days when 'sun oil' was the only thing you could smear yourself with to protect against harmful rays, Terry thought he would save some money. He'd make his own. It was only brown oil, he reasoned. So, before going on holiday his kids watched spellbound as he confidently mixed some baby oil with some brown vinegar. Just give it a shake and… no, not salad dressing, but homemade 'sun oil'. "There you go, kids," he said, proudly. "Why waste money when you can make it yourself?"

Come the holiday, come the moment when he sat on the beach and smeared himself with the concoction, smug in the knowledge that he had saved himself money. Then, taking his two kids by the hand, he strolled down to the waterfront. The next moment, Terry was frantically trying to fend off a swarm of wasps. As the kids ran away in horror, he tried batting the wasps away with his hands and kicking at them. Not surprisingly, he was stung rather badly and his yelps could be heard all over the beach. People watched in amazement as he charged towards the sea, followed by the angry swarm of bees, and hurled himself into the water.

Whether the wasps were attracted to his homemade sun block or irritated by it, he couldn't be sure. But he was sure that he was never going to use it again!

BEAM ME UP

When Rob went out to buy a new ceiling light for his son Roger's bedroom, he came back with a huge, rather expensive, one in the form of a spaceship.

Roger, of course, was delighted. Rob's wife Kristen, was appalled. Which just goes to show, thought Rob, that women have no sense of imagination. Rob set about fitting the new light and took off his glasses, placing them on the work shelf at the top of his stepladder while he attended to the fiddly close-up work of forcing wires into terminal blocks.

Then the hook that was holding the heavy light up on the ceiling gave way and the whole lot plummeted down, crashing into the top of the step ladder and smashing his glasses to pieces.

Beam me up, Scotty . . .

WISE WORDS

"It always drove me mad when my dad would say, 'You'll realise when you get older,'" Dean recalled. "It would seem such a cop-out and I was convinced that he was wrong and that I wouldn't realise anything different at all. But I must admit that I have found myself saying it to my own children, even though I know it must be as infuriating for them as it was for me!"

My mother was like a
drill sergeant. Dad was the
commanding general.

George W Bush

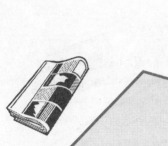
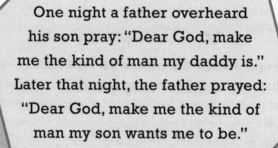

One night a father overheard
his son pray: "Dear God, make
me the kind of man my daddy is."
Later that night, the father prayed:
"Dear God, make me the kind of
man my son wants me to be."

Unknown

THAT'S LUCKY!

When Colin moved to a new village in Kent, he decided to join the local cricket team. His two young sons watched proudly as dad showed them what he could do. First off, he showed them how to catch a ball in your groin, which left them giggling as he rolled around the floor in agony.

Later he trod in some dog muck, much to the amusement of his team mates. "That's a sign of good luck!" one of them chuckled.

When it came to bat, Colin did reasonably well and even sent one ball flying out of the ground, much to his satisfaction. At the end of the game, he said goodbye and walked to his car, with his boys. But when he got there, he found his windscreen had been smashed by the ball he had hit out of the ground!

From then on, he was known by all the cricketers as 'Lucky!'

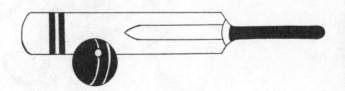

SEND IN THE CLOWN

For Tommy's fifth birthday party, mum had invited his friends over. There was great excitement as they sat around the table and the lights were switched off. Slowly, dad carried in the candle-lit cake.

Easy now. Whoops! He slipped, fell on the floor and somehow managed to bury his face slap bang in the cake. All the kids hooted with laughter. If he had tried – and he had done – he could not have been more entertaining at his son's party. He had just pulled off a pratt fall of which a professional clown would have been proud!

Who needs to pay for entertainment when you can give your son and all his friends the biggest laugh they've ever had just by falling over?

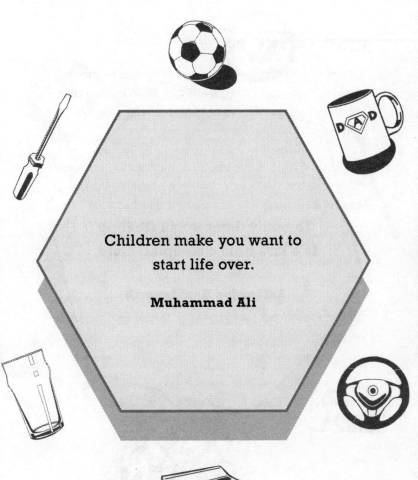

Children make you want to
start life over.

Muhammad Ali

The only thing worth stealing
is a kiss from a sleeping child.

Author Joe Houldsworth

AND NOW FOR SOME GOOD NEWS

The good news is that there are so many good things about being a dad that they far outweigh all of what you might think are bad things. In fact, some of the bad things will even turn into good things for some new dads, once they learn to appreciate the joys of fatherhood.

As a young man, you might be horrified at the prospect of carrying a child in a sling, pushing a pram or walking along the street holding hands with a toddler. Yet those are things that you may well come to enjoy. Similarly, having the back seat of your car taken up with child seats, or giving up the space in the boot previously devoted to sports bags and golf clubs for the baby's travel bag and buggy, are things that may become a source of pride rather than disappointment.

The best things about being a dad, however, will reveal themselves to every father in slightly different ways, a little at a time, every single day for the rest of your life.

I found a love I never thought
I'd find, after I had my son.

Colin Farrell

10 GOOD REASONS FOR BEING A DAD

1) You can play with soldiers, toy cars and Lego with (or without) your child.

2) Their kisses and cuddles will be priceless.

3) Just watching them asleep is so heart warming.

4) There will always be chocolate in the house for you to pinch.

5) Finishing their left-overs is a real treat.

6) Mess and nasty smells can always be blamed on your kids

7) "We were unable to get a babysitter," is a great excuse for not going somewhere you don't want to.

8) "The kids are getting tired," is a great excuse for leaving early.

9) You can catch up on all those kids' films that you missed when you were a child.

10) You suddenly seem to have a purpose in life.

THANKS, DAD!

"Train sets are wasted on children," Derek insists. "When I had a son I bought him a train set with all the bits and pieces but I was far more interested in it than him. When he lost interest I just kept going and bought more and more stuff – track, trains, people, buildings. Thankfully I had a loft to put it in.

"I know my wife thought I was turning into a bit of a 'sad case' but I would explain to her that I was doing it for my son and that he would love it when it was all done. But, of course, I was just using him as an excuse. As far as I was concerned, he could play with his own toys and I'd play with mine!"

GET THE MESSAGE?

Debbie remembers hearing her dad in the shower singing to The Police's *Message in a Bottle* – "A year has passed since I broke my nose."

When she later told him that the line was: 'A year has passed since I wrote my note,' he replied: "Oh, really? I suppose that does make more sense."

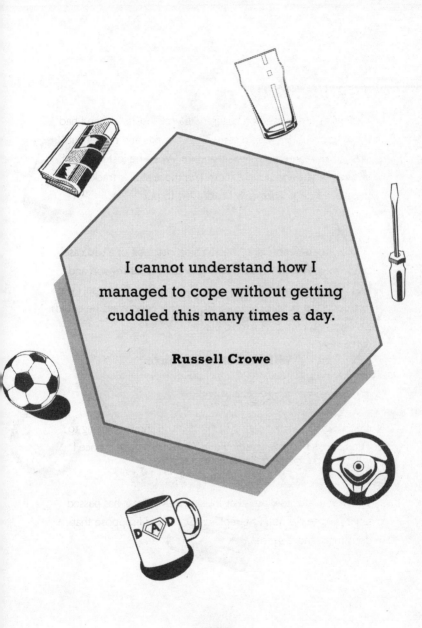

I cannot understand how I managed to cope without getting cuddled this many times a day.

Russell Crowe

When a father gives to his son, both laugh; when a son gives to his father, both cry.

William Shakespeare

WHO NEEDS SERVANTS?

"It's great when your kids reach the age where they not only want to make you breakfast in bed but can actually create something decent," says Gordon, "but you will have to endure some horrors first!

"There will be the early attempts consisting of dry bread and a glass of water. 'Mmm… That was lovely. Thanks.' It's a sweet gesture on their part but really not what you want when you wake up with a mouth as dry as the bottom of a bird cage. Other attempts may be burnt toast with a smidgen of butter or half a packet of Coco Pops swimming in an ocean of milk.

"But by the time they are old enough to be able to make a cup of coffee or tea then it's luxury. But make the most of it while it lasts because the novelty of 'breakfast surprise' soon wears off and it will be back to getting up and making your own again."

MEMO TO DADDY . . .

There's no doubt that children can melt your heart …

Terry's Monday morning blues were instantly erased when he arrived at his office and opened his briefcase to find a note inside from his nine-year-old daughter. It read, simply, 'Dear Daddy. Have a nice day!'

The greatest gift I ever had
came from God, and I call him Dad!

Anonymous

NOT NOW, DAD

"When I was a boy my parents bought me a *Scalextric* set of racing cars for Christmas and I think my dad loved it even more than me!" said Richard. "I certainly know that I was far more excited than my own son when I bought him one. I felt like we had changed roles when I would eagerly ask him if he wanted to play it with me and he would reply, 'Maybe later!'"

MAGIC MOMENTS

"There's nothing like the warm glow you feel when your child unexpectedly comes over to you and sits on your lap for a cuddle," says Jeff. "It's also lovely when they jump into your bed in the morning… so long as it's not for too long and it's not too early!"

BLACK AND WHITE

When his kids asked for Gameboys, John suddenly remembered the one that his wife had bought him years ago.

"I managed to find it, put some batteries in and was quite surprised that it still worked," he recalled. "I couldn't wait to see the kids' faces when I showed them. But I wasn't expecting their reaction to be hysterical laughter!

"They pointed at it and cried with laughter, saying, 'What's that?' How was I to know that they were much smaller these days than my 'house brick' version? But it did entertain them until I eventually bought them newer models. Even now, if their Gameboys aren't recharged or they go missing for a while, my old one is a handy stand-by – even if it does display the games in black and white!"

BROKEN IN PIECES

Kevin never realised he had an artistic temperament until he started playing with his son's Lego…

"I enjoyed Lego when I was a boy but it was quite basic in those days," he says. "It's more fun now. There are loads more different pieces for you to be creative with. But I think I may be throwing myself too much into it.

"A while ago I made a futuristic flying machine which I was very proud of. My son loved it… but not as much as me. And I confess that I felt quite upset when he broke it up to make something for himself!"

I need to learn how to be a good disciplinarian because I'm very good at winding up the kids, I'm just not good at chilling them out.

Matt Damon

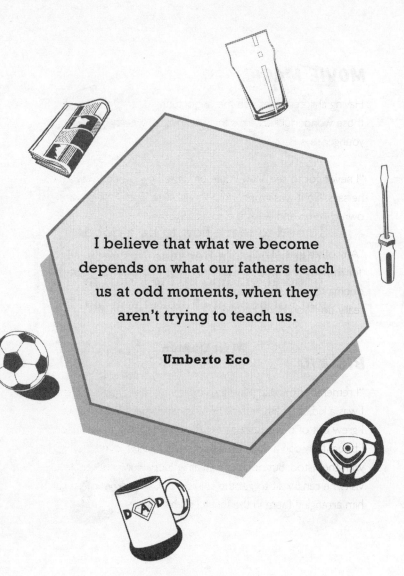

I believe that what we become depends on what our fathers teach us at odd moments, when they aren't trying to teach us.

Umberto Eco

MOVIE MAGIC

Having children gives you the opportunity to catch up on all those wonderful kids' films that you missed when you were younger, says Barry.

"I never got to see *Snow White* or *Jungle Book* when I was a kid," he says. "So it was wonderful to be able to watch them with my own children and enjoy the magic together.

"Any other kids' film that I fancy seeing, I just buy a DVD of it 'for my kids' and watch it with them. Or I'll take them to the cinema to see new releases. But it's not something you can really do if you don't have kids."

BIG KID

"I remember my dad playing soldiers with me for ages when I was a kid," says Jim. "I think he was quite disappointed when I grew out of them. But he's happy now that he's a granddad. I bought my son a fort and soldiers and found I loved playing with them, too. But not as much as granddad! Whenever he visits, he can't wait to get the soldiers out and sometimes I catch him arranging them in the fort all on his own!"

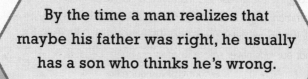

By the time a man realizes that maybe his father was right, he usually has a son who thinks he's wrong.

Charles Wadsworth

BE QUIET!

The old adage that kids 'should be seen and not heard' is, of course, terribly outdated and not something that you would ever hear any parent saying nowadays. Or is it? The simple fact that we still recognise the phrase means that it hasn't actually slipped out of common usage and, let's be honest, there are times when we all think precisely along those lines. There are times when we all wish that our kids never said a word to anyone – because no one can embarrass you quite like
your own child…

DAD'S JOKES

A dad was trying hard to get ketchup to come out of the bottle. During his struggle the phone rang, so he asked his four-year-old daughter to answer it.

"It's the vicar, Daddy!" she called. But, seeing him still, absorbed in his business, she said into the phone: "Daddy can't to talk to you right now. He's hitting the bottle."

A little boy got lost when his dad took him along to his sports club and found himself in the women's locker room. When he was spotted, the room burst into shrieks, with ladies grabbing towels and running for cover. The little boy watched in amazement and then asked, "What's the matter. Haven't you ever seen a little boy before?"

On her first day at school, Samantha handed her teacher a note from her father which read: "The opinions expressed by this child are not necessarily those of her parents."

Don't hold your parents up to contempt. After all, you are their son, and it is just possible that you may take after them.

Evelyn Waugh

The truth is that parents are not really interested in justice. They just want quiet.

Bill Cosby

TIME TO GO

Dennis took his four-year-old daughter, Nicki, to a toy shop where she made a bee-line for the cuddly animals. One in particular left her wide-eyed in wonderment. It was a five-foot high Labrador Retriever puppy just like the one she had seen in the TV commercials for Andrex toilet tissue.

As Dennis tried to move her away, she shouted at the top of her voice, "I want the Durex puppy now!"

TOUPEE OR NOT TOUPEE

Tony was speechless when he was walking around in a shopping centre with his 12-year-old daughter and they saw a man approaching them, wearing an obvious toupee.

"She looked at him and casually remarked, 'You don't think that looks natural, do you?'" he recalls.

"I don't know who was the most embarrassed – him or me. Neither of us knew what to say and so we just carried on walking!"

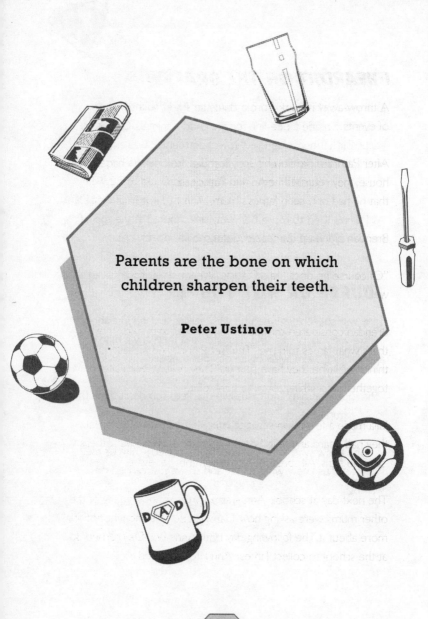

Parents are the bone on which
children sharpen their teeth.

Peter Ustinov

I HEARD IT ON THE GRAPEVINE . . .

A throw-away remark from a child can set off a chain
of events….

After Patrick picked up his son, Brendan, from his friend James's
house, they returned home and Patrick remarked to his wife
that he had only seen James's mum, Ann, but not his father, Dan.

Brendan piped up, "James's dad doesn't live with his mum."

"Of course he does," said Patrick. "We know his parents quite
well."

Brendan considered this for a moment and then said, "Well,
that's what James told me." That set Patrick and his wife Julia,
thinking. Maybe they have split up? They haven't been seen
together for a while, come to think of it.

Julia made a few phone calls to other 'school mums' to see if
they had heard anything. Some expressed surprise but others
'saw the signs.' All spread it further on the grapevine.

The next day at school, Ann was surprised at how many of the
other mums were asking how Dan was. But she thought nothing
more about it. The following day, both Anne *and* Dan turned up
at the school to collect James. Ann later confided

to Julia that James had been telling a lot of lies, lately. She's still unaware that one of his lies caused such a stir!

WHO'S DADDY?

Whenever she was asked her name, Jessica would reply, "I'm Mr. Brown's daughter." Her mother told her this was wrong, and that she should say, "I'm Jessica Brown." At church, the following Sunday, the smiling vicar asked her, "Aren't you Mr. Brown's daughter?" Jessica replied, "I thought I was, but mother says I'm not."

NO ONE WILL EVER KNOW!

To avoid paying for his five kids when they went to a theme park, Bill smuggled his youngest two in under the parcel shelf in the back of the car. But he was mortified when he went to parents' evening at his son's school and spoke to his teacher who told him that she had asked the class to relate what they had done during the summer holidays and Bill's son had told the entire class of his car boot adventure!

An angry father is most cruel towards himself.

Writer of Latin maxims, Publilius Syrus

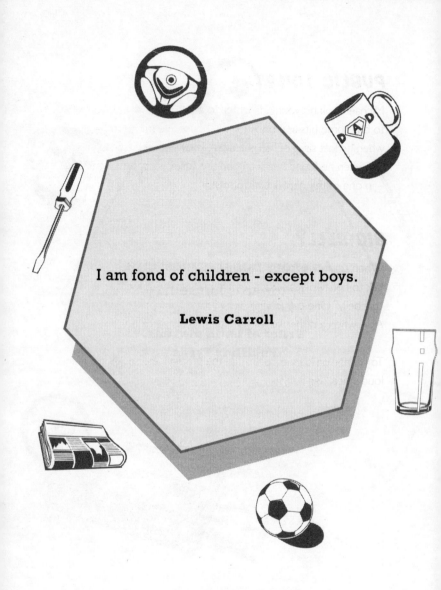

I am fond of children - except boys.

Lewis Carroll

PUBLIC TOILET

Michael took his young daughter to a DIY store at the weekend to buy some bits and bobs for the house. He began to panic when he lost sight of her but didn't know whether to laugh or cry when he found her sitting on the toilet doing a 'number two' – in one of the display bathrooms!

BIG BELLY

When Laura was pregnant with her second child, she used to talk to her two-year-old daughter Joanne, about the size of her "big belly." One day Joanne went to the library with her dad, Alan, when a rather large woman entered.

To his horror, Joanne pointed at the woman and said in really loud voice, "Big belly!"

TOILET TROUBLE

Graham will never forget the time when he took his small son, Tim, to the toilet in a restaurant and Tim shouted, "Daddy let go of my penis!"

He recalls: "I was just so embarrassed when I came out, knowing that everyone had heard. Goodness knows what they thought of me."

SILLY BILLY

Dave took his two young daughters to the park and, as they were enjoying themselves on the roundabout, they saw another man walk too close to the swings and get kicked in the chest by the girl sitting on the swing. He wasn't hurt but looked embarrassed and Dave couldn't stop his girls from giggling.

They labelled him "Silly Billy" and couldn't wait to get home and tell Mummy about the funny man. But a few days later, it was Dave's turn to be embarrassed. He was walking along the street with his girls behind a man carrying his groceries in a plastic carrier bag. When the bag split, milk and bread fell out and various tins rolled away from him.

"Look, Dad!" shrieked his youngest daughter. "It's Silly Billy!"

Dining out with kids is brilliant.
They're the cheapest dates around.
They never order the lobster.

David Letterman

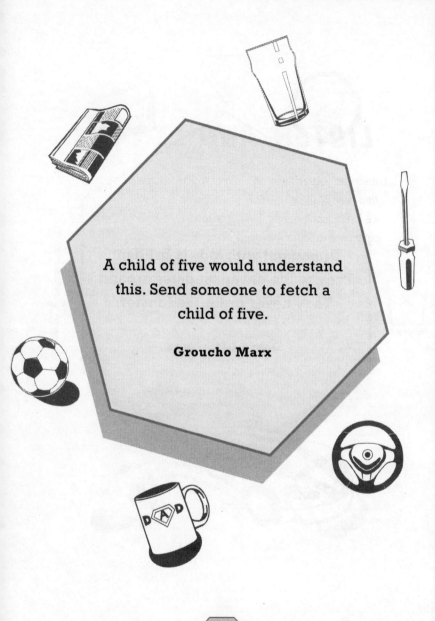

A child of five would understand this. Send someone to fetch a child of five.

Groucho Marx

LISTEN AND LEARN

*Listening to your children, and also to your own father, is something
that none of us do as much as we should. But if we don't, then
we lose valuable insight and understanding. Your own father has
experience to share with you, if you only ask. And a young child's
unexpected wisdom can be staggering.*

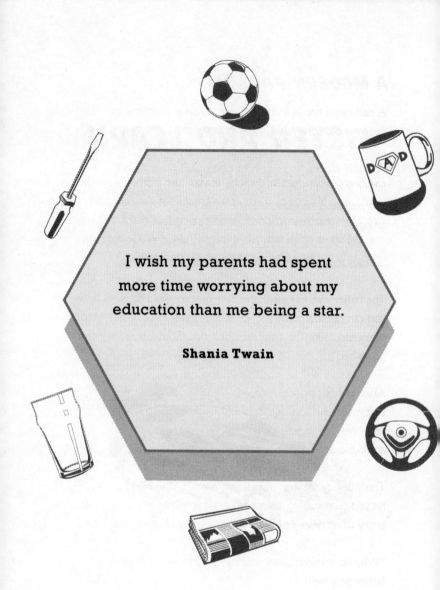

I wish my parents had spent
more time worrying about my
education than me being a star.

Shania Twain

A MODERN PARABLE

A dad came home from work late, tired and irritated, to find his five-year-old son waiting for him at the door.

"Daddy," said his son. "How much do you make an hour?" His father told him that it was none of his business but when his son persisted, he replied, "If you must know, I make £20 an hour."

"Daddy, may I please borrow £10?" said his son.

The father was furious. "If the only reason you asked that is so you can borrow some money to buy a silly toy or some other nonsense, then you march yourself straight to your room and go to bed.."

After an hour or so the man had calmed down and thought that maybe his son, who had never asked for money before, really needed to buy something. He went up to his room to apologise and handed him £10.

The little boy sat straight up and smiled. "Oh, thank you, Daddy!" he said, then started counting out all his money. His father was angry when he saw how much his son already had.

"Why do you want more money if you already have some?" his father grumbled.

"Because I didn't have enough, but now I do," the little boy replied. "Daddy, I have £20 now. Can I buy an hour of your time? Please come home early tomorrow. I would like to have dinner with you."

The father was crushed. He put his arms around his son, and begged for his forgiveness.

OF COURSE, CHILDREN TALK COMPLETE NONSENSE, TOO...

Four-year-old James was listening to a Bible story. His dad read, "The man named Lot was warned to take his wife and flee out of the city but his wife looked back and was turned to salt." Concerned, James asked, "What happened to the flea?"

A father was in church with his three-year-old daughter, Lizzie, watching a baby being baptised. As the vicar poured water over the tot's head, Lizzie turned to her dad and said, "Daddy, why is he brainwashing that baby?"

A young lad was walking along the beach with his father when they came upon a dead seagull in the sand. "Daddy, what happened to him?" the son asked. "He died and went to Heaven," his father replied. The boy thought a moment and then said, "Did God throw him back down?"

A three-year-old boy went with his dad to see a new litter of kittens. On returning home, he breathlessly informed his mother, "There were two boy kittens and two girl kittens." "How did you know that?" his mother asked. "Daddy picked them up and looked underneath," he replied. "I think it's printed on the bottom."

THANK GOD

A small boy was wide-eyed at the fireworks display at Walt Disney World, Florida, as he sat on his father's shoulders.

As the last of the fireworks lit up the skies, he said, "Thank you, God."

A father was listening to his child saying his prayers but was puzzled when he began, "Dear Harold." Dad interrupted asking, "Wait a minute. Why are you calling God 'Harold'"?

The little boy looked up and said, "That's what they call him in church. You know the prayer we say, "Our Father, who art in Heaven, Harold be Thy Name."

Children have neither past nor future; they enjoy the present.

French writer Jean de la Bruyere

When you want something
expensive, ask your grandparents.

Matthew, age 12

BEING THERE

"One of my first memories growing up was wishing that my father would be home more," said a dad from Sacramento, California. "I was eight, and we had just returned from a canoe trip. I remember thinking, 'I don't want a bigger house or more money. I just want my dad around.'"

PIG TALE

"One evening my young daughter was running around when she stubbed her toes on the dresser," says Ross. "She cried out, grabbing her foot and sank to the floor. I rushed to her side and asked where it hurt. She looked at me through tear-filled eyes and managed to moan, 'It's the piggy that ate all the roast beef.'"

Love is what's in the room with you at Christmas if you stop opening presents and listen.

Bobby, age 7

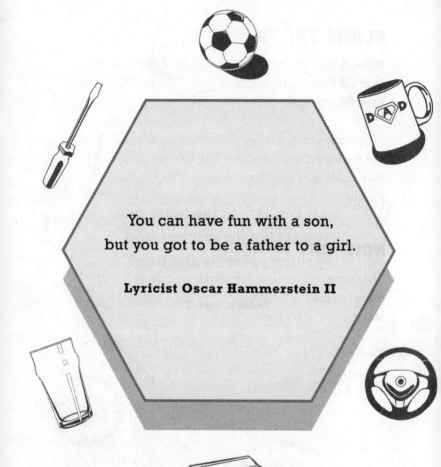

You can have fun with a son,
but you got to be a father to a girl.

Lyricist Oscar Hammerstein II

BLAME THE FATHER

Britney Spears was dumbstruck after hearing her young sons, Sean and Preston, uttering bad language. She blamed the father, Kevin Ferderline, aka rapper K-Fed.

"The kids are starting to learn words like 'stupid' and Preston says the f-word now sometimes," she said. "He doesn't get it from us. He must get it from his daddy. I say it, but not around my kids."

NOW, SAY IT AGAIN

The mother of actor and comedian Sanjeev Bhaskar, once found his father by Sanjeev's cot, chanting, "I want to be a businessman," in his sleeping ear.

Later, when Sanjeev announced he wanted to be an actor, his dad replied: "It's pronounced 'doctor'"

When your dad is mad and
asks you, "Do I look stupid?"
don't answer.

Hannah, age 9

DAD, YOU'RE SOOOOOOOOO EMBARRASSING

Better face up to it, you are going to be an embarrassment to your kids. Remember when your parents made you cringe every now and then? Well, what makes you so cool? And there's nothing more un-cool than a dad trying to be cool. In time, your kids will blush less easily and deal with your mortifying exploits with a simple look of disgust. But, no matter how old the child becomes, the father's gift to embarrass is ever there, ready to be brought out at a moment's notice.

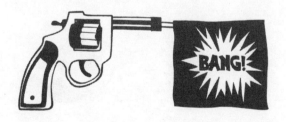

LIKE FATHER, LIKE SON

Ewan McGregor's proud parents enjoyed watching his latest movies at the cinema but the actor was worried about them seeing his nude scenes in the risqué movie *The Pillow Book*.

He hesitantly suggested to his father that they might want to give this particular film a miss but a few days later he received a fax from his parents saying that they thought it was a beautiful film. At the bottom his dad had added: 'PS. I'm glad to see you've inherited one of my major assets.'

BRA WARS

Rolling Stone Keith Richards was shocked by how quickly his daughter grew up. "You go out on the road for a couple of months, come back, and suddenly Jayne Mansfield's standing there and you're tripping over training bras," he said. "That can kill you. They just fling them anywhere!"

I don't think my parents know
what I do.

John Malkovich

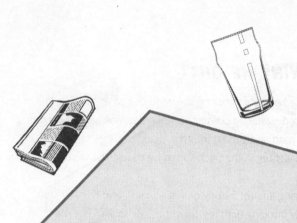

You know your children are
growing up when they stop asking
you where they came from and
refuse to tell you where
they're going.

P. J. O'Rourke

FREAKIN' ME OUT!

Kids have a knack of knocking the wind out of your sails with their often devastating comments. One dad was happily driving along the road and getting into the swing of things with his four-year-old daughter, in the back. Or so he thought…

"I was singing *If You're Happy and You Know It* and thinking that I was really bonding with my daughter," he recalls. "But she suddenly piped up, 'Um… Dad? You're kind of um… freakin' me out!'"

THANKS, DAD!

Family nicknames may be okay at home but leave them behind when you close the front door. Poor Robyn blushed bright red when her dad picked her up from school, hugged her in front of her friends and called her Poppet. From then on all her classmates called her Poppet.

HOLLYWOOD IDIOT

Hollywood actor Adam Sandler's dad took things into his own hands when he despaired at him ever being able to write clearly.

"My parents had their telephone number in the phone book and so they would get lots of calls from kids wanting my autograph," Adam recalls. "My father rang me once and said, 'I got a list of 250 kids and they want your autograph.' But when I told him to send me the list he replied, 'No, it's okay, I already signed them for you.' I was appalled and said, 'You can't do that, dad!' And he just explained, 'You're handwriting's terrible!'

"So, I was in New Hampshire and this kid came up to me and said, 'Thank you for the autograph.' When I looked at it, I saw written, 'Dear Benny. I should have taken the garbage out when my mother asked me to. I am garbage for not taking out the garbage. I think I'm so great 'cause I'm rich. I suck! Love, the Hollywood idiot, Adam Sandler!'"

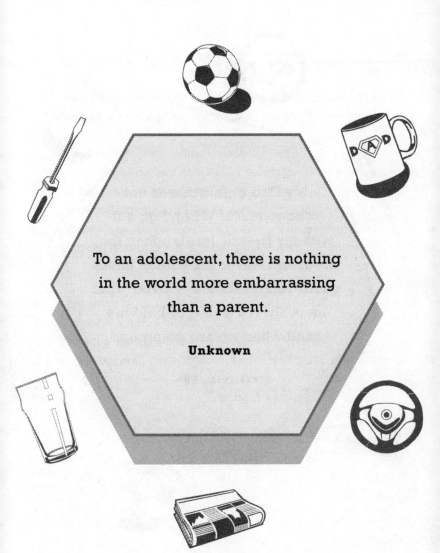

To an adolescent, there is nothing
in the world more embarrassing
than a parent.

Unknown

My Dad embarrasses me sooooo much! When I go out with my friends he stands in the street and waves his hankie to say goodbye and shouts "Olivia!" And he is always trying to hold my hand when we are going out!

Olivia, 10

10 THINGS A CHILD WILL NEVER HEAR A DAD SAY...

1) "Why don't you have a tattoo done?"

2) "That's a very nice short skirt you are wearing."

3) "I seem to be lost. We'll have to stop and ask for directions."

4) "Here's my credit card. Now go and enjoy yourself."

5) "I'd rather you gave up football and concentrated on ballet lessons."

6) "Your mother and I are going away for the weekend... you might want to consider throwing a party."

7) "I'll just lift up the car bonnet, look at the engine and touch a few things until someone takes pity on me and tells me what's wrong with it."

8) "Here, you take the TV remote."

9) "I wouldn't bother getting a job just yet. I make enough money for you to live on."

10) "Wow! What a tidy room."

WILD HORSES WON'T STOP HIM

He may have been cool as a young rock star but it's good to know that Mick Jagger is just another embarrassing dad.

When his kids have parties he likes to dig out some of the flamboyant clothes he wore in the 60s and 70s.

"They think I'm a bit funny sometimes – and not funny ha-ha – but that's all right," says Mick. "I like to dress up when they have parties and they look at me and groan, 'Oh, Dad!' I always think I look sharp but when I come downstairs you can see their faces change colour!"

MEET AND GREET

US President Barack Obama is just another cringe-worthy dad at heart. His 10-year-old daughter, Malia, recalls the time when her friend came over during the election campaign when her father – still in campaign mode – shook the girl's hand to say hello. Malia told him, "You don't shake kids' hands that much. You just wave or say hi."

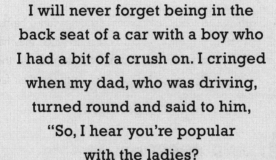

I will never forget being in the back seat of a car with a boy who I had a bit of a crush on. I cringed when my dad, who was driving, turned round and said to him, "So, I hear you're popular with the ladies?

Samantha, 13

I'll probably be one of those very embarrassing parents who's a naturist.

Robbie Williams

WHAT AN ATHLETE!

What is it that makes usually sloth-like men think they are Olympic competitors when it comes to the Dads' Race at School Sports Day?

Never mind that their daily exercise routine consists of walking to the car or lifting a beer can, this is 'The Big One' and there's no shortage of competitors. Forget the Mums' Race. That's a fun stroll in the park. There might be some nervous laughter as the dads take to the track but, make no mistake, this is deadly serious. The fear of being last is terrifying.

The smell of testosterone fills the air as these 'super athletes' jostle for position on the starting line. Focussed now and flicking their feet like they've seen sprinters do on the telly, they are as oblivious to their pot bellies as they are their giggling children and startled wives.

And they're off! If you've never seen a herd of stampeding rhinos up close, well this is the next best thing. Red faced and puffing, shoving and charging, it's a terrifying sight. The ground shakes, one or two fall and someone at the back pretends to have a hamstring injury so he can pull out without being thought of as 'last.' At the other end of the track there's a flurry of arms, legs and bellies as the front runners crash through the finishing tape and, unable to stop, knock over the trophy table.

That's it. All over. Put your feet up, Dad. You've done your bit. Same again next year.

DADS UNITED

For those competitive dads who can't wait for the annual School Sports Day Dads' Race, there's the Parents' Football Team. Having watched their sons playing football from the sidelines, abused the opposition and heckled the ref, they have decided to find their old footie boots and grace the field once more.

Convinced that 'the old magic is still there,' (even if it never was) they mostly stand around waiting for the ball to come to them and occasionally lurch into a 'run' which leaves them breathless and gagging for a cigarette.

Dad in a football kit is a disturbing spectacle for children. And it's a memory that will never leave them.

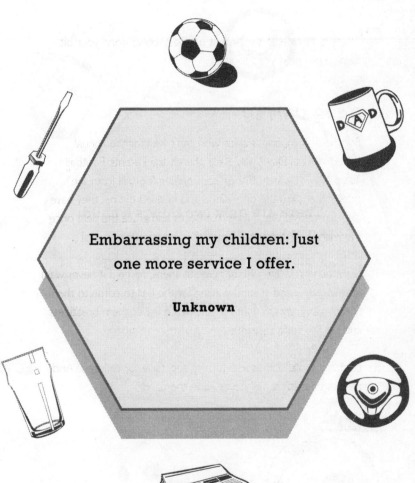

Embarrassing my children: Just one more service I offer.

Unknown

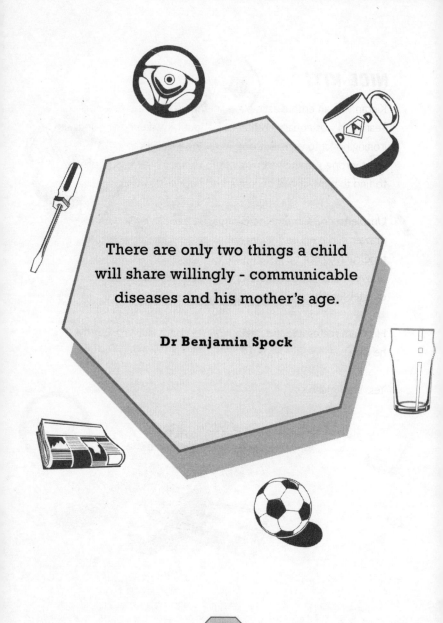

There are only two things a child will share willingly - communicable diseases and his mother's age.

Dr Benjamin Spock

NICE KIT!

Kieran was an enthusiastic player in the School Parents' Football Team and was equally enthusiastic about his wife washing and ironing his kit for him. But one week this 'ideal' arrangement went wrong. On the morning of the big match he was horrified to find that his kit had been washed but was still sopping wet.

Unable to dry it in time he rummaged through every clothes drawer in the house, looking for something else to wear. With time running out he became increasingly desperate and ended up wearing a yellow T-shirt, a pair of tennis socks and three-quarter length camouflage shorts!

His team mates and the opposition fell about laughing. But did he care?

Yes. Very much so.

DISCO DAD

Eat your heart out John Travolta. Usually seen at wedding, birthday or anniversary parties where he can make the most of a large and shiny dance floor, Disco Dad is summoned by the opening bars of a funky beat.

He's out of his chair and shakin' his thang in a trance-like state before he even reaches the dance floor. The shoulders are doing most of the work. There's a strange chicken-like walk and a rather camp wiggling of hips. He's punching the air with one hand and holding his beer in the other. And then he's there. On the dance floor. Under the spotlight. Shirt hanging out of his trousers and plastered to his perspiring back. Shiny of face, grinning like a mad man and looking around to see who is going to join him.

We've all been there…. or will be. At some stage. It's part of being a dad. A rite of passage. The wise will get it over and done with as soon as possible and then watch the video prior to any subsequent wedding, birthday or anniversary bash as a reminder not to do it again – then they'll probably do it again, anyway. It's the beat. It's the groove. It's the booze…

DISCO DAD TOP 10

Here they are. Named and shamed. Just the opening bars of any of these songs should be taken as danger signs for kids everywhere. Run and hide for Dad is about to get down on it....

1. *Oops Upside Your Head* – The Gap Band

2. *YMCA* – Village People

3. *Night Fever* – Bee Gees

4. *You're The First, The Last, My Everything* – Barry White

5. *Celebration* – Kool & The Gang

6. *You Sexy Thing* – Hot Chocolate

7. *Brown Girl In The Ring* – Boney M

8. *Get Down On It* – Kool & The Gang

9. *Le Freak* – Chic

10. *Billie Jean* – Michael Jackson

PROUD TO BE COWARD

Alison will never forget going on holiday with her parents when she was a teenager. Dad decided on a pre-dinner drink in the hotel bar and was delighted to find a pianist entertaining the handful of people there. After a drink or two he got into the swing of things and sauntered over to the pianist and asked her if she knew any Noel Coward tunes. To Alison's horror she heard her dad singing *Mad Dogs and Englishmen*, whilst casually leaning on the piano in what he assumed was a debonair fashion.

THANKS, DAD!

Father-of-seven Rod Stewart made his daughter, Ruby, blush when she was 19 by saying she had too much attitude to make it in music.

"She's got a great voice but she's a little cocky and doesn't want to learn from her old dad," said her old dad. "Ruby marches to the beat of her own drum and won't listen to me. She'll find out the hard way eventually."

This came after he had made his older daughter, Kimberly, cringe by talking publicly about her liver troubles, saying they were brought on by boozing.

Having one child makes you a parent;
having two you are a referee.

David Frost

Every father should remember
that one day his son will follow his
example instead of his advice

Unknown

INAPPROPRIATE BEHAVIOUR

1. Fancying your son's girlfriends.

2. Getting frisky with your wife in front of the children.

3. Laughing when your children are rude.

4. Walking around the house naked.

5. Leaving the toilet door open.

6. Road rage.

7. Arm wrestling your daughter's boyfriend.

8. Playing pranks with a whoopee cushion.

9. Falling over drunk.

10. Breaking wind.

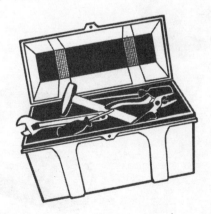

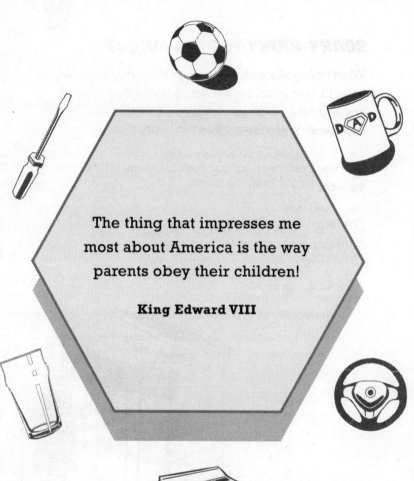

The thing that impresses me
most about America is the way
parents obey their children!

King Edward VIII

SCARY HAIRY

When Hollwood actor Kevin Bacon picked up his daughter, Sosie, 13, from school, she was shocked at his appearance. He was wearing hair extensions that he wore for his role as snooty salon owner Jorge in *Beauty Shop*.

"She was totally mortified," says Kevin, whose wife, Kyra, loved the locks.

"We're very embarrassing parents," he admits. "We're constantly humiliating our kids in public."

HAIL THE MIGHTY MADELEY

TV chat show host Richard Madeley is King of Embarrassing Dads. When he's not talking publicly about his and wife Judy's sex life, he's discussing the intimate details of his long-suffering children. Richard has the unnerving knack of saying anything that comes into his head. And he tries way too hard to be 'down there with the kids.'

Over the years he has shared with us everything from how he once took Viagra to spice up his love life, to how his teenaged daughter Chloe was coping with her first period.

Richard's classic Ali G impression – "Is it cos I is black?" – was one of the most cringe-making moments on TV.

"My brother, Jack, who was then 13, desperately tried to convince Dad not to do it," says Chloe, 20. "He stormed off to bed when he realised that if our father wants to do something, he will do it."

How very true.

Another jaw dropping moment was when Richard broke off midway through his chat show to look into the camera and say: "I would just like to make a gesture at this point to the person who stole my daughter's mobile phone." To the disbelief of everyone watching, he then shook his fist in an 'angry' fashion! Enough? Sadly, he was just warming up. Easing 'seamlessly' into teen-speak, he explained that Chloe had been "jacked on the street." As is usual at moments like this, an increasingly embarrassed Judy slapped him on the knee to shut him up.

But never let it be said that he's simply playing up to the camera. Oh, no. He's like it at home, too. "At home, Dad is exactly as he is on TV - bad impressions and awful jokes included," complains Chloe. "He is just as frank and direct as he is on his show. He will start talking about contraception or sex at the dinner table, for example.

"When I was younger I found it a lot harder to deal with some of the topics my parents talked about on their show. As a happily married couple they do have sex and would often talk about it. But no child wants to hear about their parents' sex life and I would cringe when someone mentioned something they had said.

"I could not ask for more supportive, loving and understanding parents - but I wish they would behave."

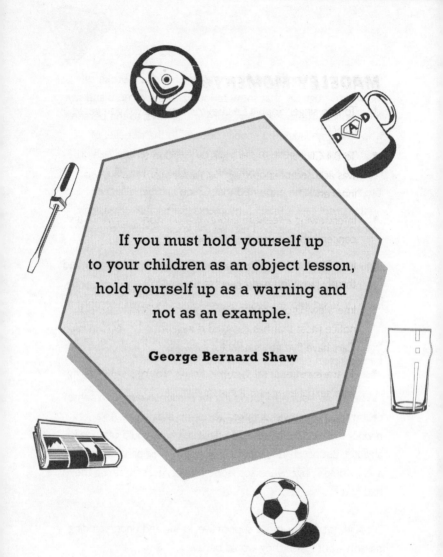

If you must hold yourself up
to your children as an object lesson,
hold yourself up as a warning and
not as an example.

George Bernard Shaw

MADELEY MOMENTS

* To pop singer Sophie Ellis Bextor: "Where did you get your face?"

* To Bill Clinton: "I was in a similar position to you. I was accused of shoplifting. But unlike you, I knew I was innocent."

* Interviewing a teenage anorexic: "Five stone? Wow! That's concentration camp thin, that is."

* In an item about menstruation: "Remember when you had thrush, Judy? You had a terrible time of it."

* Interviewing one of the Birmingham Six: "What do you notice most that has changed during your 18 years in jail? Cars have five gears now, for example."

* To transvestite artist Grayson Perry: "You're just humming with sexual energy! Is it the fabric?"

* "I love ducks - they've always got a smile on their face."

In America there are two
classes of travel - first class,
and with children.

Robert Benchley

DISCIPLINE

"Spare the road and spoil the child," is a phrase that should, of course, be consigned to the Dark Ages. This chapter is simply about bringing your child up to have respect, discipline and manners. And if you can manage to do that then it's no mean achievement. Because it's not easy…

I DIDN'T DO IT

Sometimes it's best not to waste your breath, says Frank. "If two or more children are in a room and you hear a crash or one of them crying there is absolutely no point in rushing in and asking, 'Who did it?'" he insists. "Only the truly naïve will expect somebody to say, 'I did.' In reality, they will reply, one after another, 'I didn't do it.'"

WHOOPS!

Craig was mightily embarrassed when his son's school teacher told him that when she had asked young Trevor, "What comes after three?" he had innocently replied,
"A smack."

No man needs a vacation so
much as the man who has
just had one.

Elbert Hubbard

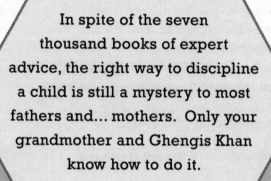

In spite of the seven thousand books of expert advice, the right way to discipline a child is still a mystery to most fathers and... mothers. Only your grandmother and Ghengis Khan know how to do it.

Bill Cosby

NAUGHTY STAIR

Celebrity couple David and Victoria Beckham seem to have their feet on the ground when it comes to home life. Despite their wealth, they are determined not to let their children become spoilt brats.

"I am quite strict, believe it or not, in every way," says David. "We have the naughty stair at home and if the boys have been naughty they sit on the second step of the stairs. If we're somewhere else, they'll sit on a naughty chair. I'm very strong on respect. I bring my sons up to show respect to people. They will never get anything unless they have said 'please' or 'thank you'. I absolutely make sure of that and so does Victoria."

I CAN'T WAIT!

"Just you wait 'til your father gets home!" said an angry Jeannie after her daughter had been a little horror for most of the day.

"Can we go and pick him up from work?" she replied, eagerly.

FLARE-UP

Actor Kevin Spacey admits to being a difficult child, growing up in California. At the age of 14 his parents shipped him off to military academy following a domestic fracas.

"I won't tell you exactly what the incident was that made my parents send me to military school," he later said. "Let's just say it involved my sister's tree-house and some matches."

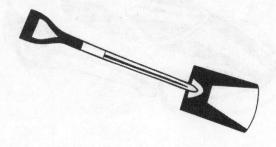

The father who does not teach
his son his duties is equally guilty
with the son who neglects them.

Confucius

I won't have my kids getting lippy. No swearing. I don't smack either. I give them a dropped eyebrow look and then they know.

Liam Gallagher

THAT SMELLS GOOD

Rob walked into the bathroom to find that his five-year-old son, Sam, had tipped several bottles of bubble bath, shampoo and moisturiser into the bath.

"What on earth are you doing?" asked Rob.

"There's too many bottles," Sam replied. "I thought I'd just mix them all together."

FEAR OF FLYING

In August 2002, a 12-year-old boy developed a flying phobia while on holiday in Ireland. Not a problem if you happen to live in the UK, but his family had to get him home to Sao Paolo, in Brazil.

His father spent thousands on hypnotism and tranquilisers to get him on a plane, but to no avail. Eventually he had to travel across land and water, finally sailing home from Genoa in Italy.

The journey took 20 days.

MELTING AWAY

American author and broadcaster Garrison Keillor knows that daughters have their fathers wrapped around their little finger...

"The father of a daughter is nothing but a high-class hostage," he says. "A father turns a stony face to his sons, berates them, shakes his antlers, paws the ground, snorts, runs them off into the underbrush, but when his daughter puts her arm over his shoulder and says, 'Daddy, I need to ask you something,' he is a pat of butter in a hot frying pan."

LOW EXPECTATIONS

Actor and comedian Sanjeev Bhaskar takes a modest approach to bringing up his son. "Maybe the best thing we can do is to make sure that they are a slight improvement on us."

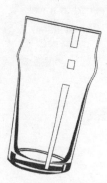

All children alarm their parents,
if only because you are forever
expecting to encounter yourself.

Gore Vidal

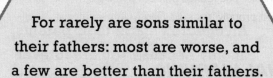

For rarely are sons similar to their fathers: most are worse, and a few are better than their fathers.

Homer (No, you idiot. Not that one. The Greek poet)

WORK OF ART

Grant was horrified to find his three-year-old daughter,
Stephanie, drawing on the living-room wall.

"I didn't want to tell her off because I knew she didn't realise
she was doing wrong," he said. "So I took a deep breath to calm
myself and then said, 'I don't think you meant to do that, did you,
Stephanie?' She looked at me with a big smile on her face and
replied, proudly, 'Yes, I did, Daddy!'"

FINAL WARNING

"I am not going to tell you again!" shouted an exasperated
Neil, after he had repeatedly asked his children Matthew and
Elizabeth to stop throwing toys around the room.

But as he made his way out of the room he heard Matthew
whisper to his sister, "It's okay. He's not going to tell us, again."

LIKE FATHER, LIKE SON

Actor and humourist Peter Ustinov once received a letter from the headmaster at his young son's school saying that the boy had assumed the unfortunate role of class clown and that his antics made classmates laugh and were a distraction. He ended the letter by hinting that Peter should control his child better.

Peter promptly dashed off a letter replying that he was able to afford the school's exorbitant fees, only because he was so well compensated for assuming a very similar role.

A child who is allowed to be disrespectful to his parents will not have true respect for anyone.

Billy Graham

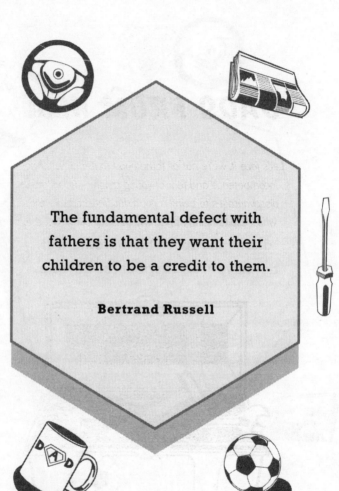

The fundamental defect with
fathers is that they want their
children to be a credit to them.

Bertrand Russell

DADS FROM HELL

Let's face it, we're not all fatherhood material. Selfishness, incompetence and fear of young children are all major disadvantages to being a good dad. Yet there are those who, despite being appallingly bad, still think that they are role models.

I'M OFF!

Convict Byron Perkins was dubbed 'the worst dad in the world' when he callously let down his son, Destin, in his hour of need.

Byron spent most of his son's childhood in prison and had recently been banged up again on drugs and weapons charges. But when Destin had a life-threatening kidney condition, he thought his dad would come good in the end. A judge was touched when Byron said that he wanted to donate a kidney and he was let out of prison. But instead of heading for hospital he fled to Mexico with his girlfriend.

Not surprisingly, Destin, 17, said he would never forgive him. "This was his final chance to step up and be a dad and he turns around and does something like that," he said. "It's not something I'm ever going to forget."

THE GRASS IS ALWAYS GREENER...

Kids have a habit of putting you in your place, even when you are England footballing hero, Gary Lineker.

"My son, George, looked at me one day and said: 'Wouldn't it be great to have David Beckham as your dad?'" he recalls. "When I asked why, he replied, 'Because he's so good at football!'"

It is easier for a father to have children than for children to have a real father.

Pope John XXIII

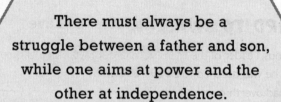

There must always be a
struggle between a father and son,
while one aims at power and the
other at independence.

Samuel Johnson

JUST TERRIBLE

In 1581, Ivan The Terrible beat his pregnant daughter-in-law for wearing immodest clothing, which may have caused a miscarriage. His son, Ivan Jnr, was incensed when he heard what had happened but Ivan Snr put a stop to the heated argument by striking him in the head with his pointed staff, causing his son's accidental death.

HARD TO SWALLOW

Cronus, Leader of the Titans from Greek mythology, learned that he was destined to be overthrown by his son, just as he had overthrown his father. To prevent the prophecy from happening, he swallowed his children Hera, Hades, Hestia, and Poseidon as soon as they were born. But his son, Zeus, who managed to avoid being eaten, later forced him to disgorge the other siblings. Hurrah!

ROLE MODEL

A father from Winnipeg insisted he was a role model to his son, despite using him as an accomplice for a botched robbery. He admitted to getting his 16-year-old son out of bed to be his "drinking buddy" and, after a boozy session, they went out with a shotgun that he had bought the previous day to protect his son against gang members.

When they spotted a group of men with a case of beer they decided to steal it at gunpoint. However, the men refused to hand it over and began struggling with the father. His son fired the shotgun at one of the men but it missed him and hit his dad in the chest. He was rushed to hospital, where he spent several weeks recovering before being locked up for four years.

He later made the jaw-dropping comment: "Despite this incident, I see myself as a role model for my son."

LIKE FATHER, LIKE SON

One summer evening during a violent thunderstorm a mother was tucking her nervous son into bed. She was about to turn off the light when he asked, "Mummy, will you sleep with me tonight?"

She gave him a hug and replied, "'I can't, dear. I have to sleep in Daddy's room."

There was a pause before the boy sneered, "The big sissy."

YOU KNOW THERE'S A TEENAGER IN THE HOUSE WHEN...

BOYS

Your razor is clogged

You wonder who that man is talking downstairs

His bedroom door is now fully closed

The smile is replaced by a scowl

His speech deteriorates into a series of grunt and mumbles

He no longer wants to play games with you

Everything you say is wrong

You never 'understand' him

His unconditional love is replaced by embarrassment

He just wants to left alone

GIRLS

She spends the morning in the bathroom

She seems unable to hear you

You worry about what she is wearing

You can't keep up with her mood swings

Your telephone bill increases

Tubes and jars of cream on the bathroom shelf multiply

You hear what she is saying but don't understand it

Her sulks last even longer than before

Her mobile phone is her constant companion

She treats you like the household imbecile

Panic, chaos, disorder...
my work here is done.

Unknown

MOVIE MONSTERS

ANAKIN SKYWALKER - STAR WARS

His idea of fatherly advice? "There is no escape. Don't make me destroy you." Well, no 'World's Best Dad' mug for *you*, on Father's Day.

He nearly strangled to death his pregnant wife and never visited his kids Luke and Leia. Later, having become Darth Vader, he kidnapped rebellious Leia for daring to question his dodgy dealings as enforcer of the Galactic Empire. During a fierce battle with Luke he cut off his hand before revealing that he was his father. To be fair, he did follow up with a job offer – ruling the galaxy as father and son.

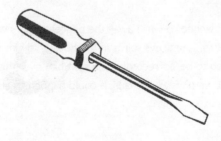

DR EVIL - AUSTIN POWERS: INTERNATIONAL MAN OF MYSTERY

There's no denying it, ambitions for world dominance get in the way of being a good dad. Dr Evil was appalled by his son Scott's lack of evilness while Scott just thought his dad a fool. In an effort to improve their relationship Evil agreed to attend group therapy with Scott. But it went pear-shaped when he 'liquidated' everyone in the group.

JACK TORRANCE - THE SHINING

There's nothing like chasing your son around with an axe for a bit of father-son bonding. Jack wasn't always a psychopath, though. It was the voices, you see.

There was a time when he considered the pen to be mightier than the sword and, being a family man, took his wife and son Danny with him when he was asked to be the caretaker of an empty hotel.

Here, he planned to while away the peaceful hours with some creative writing, until evil spirits in the hotel told him that his family need to be 'corrected' which sent him over the edge. So, you see, it wasn't really his fault. It could happen to any of us.

LESTER BURNHAM – AMERICAN BEAUTY

After attending a cheerleader competition at his daughter Jane's high school, Lester falls in lust with her flirtatious friend, Angela. His mid-life crisis sees him quitting his well-paid job to work at a fast food restaurant and re-living his youth by lifting weights, doing pot and lusting after Angela.

I won't lie to you, fatherhood isn't easy - like motherhood.

Homer Simpson

HOMER SIMPSON MOMENTS

Former US President George Bush Snr declared, "We need a nation closer to The Waltons *than* The Simpsons.

But is Homer Simpson such a bad dad? Yes, he's selfish, childish, irresponsible, negligent, eats and drinks to excess and could hardly be considered a role model to his kids. So, yes, it could be said that he is a bad dad. On the plus side… erm… he does love his family, he spends time with them and likes to make his kids laugh when they are feeling down. And… well, that's about it, really.

But his bumbling, buffoonish behaviour is an endearing quality and one that we all share from time to time.

I TOLD YOU

Dave thought he'd teach his daughter Catherine the dangers of touching a light bulb. "It gets very hot and will give you a nasty burn," he said, all fatherly-like. Unfortunately, he thought he'd press the point further and lifted her up near the light bulb for a closer look. She reached out, touched it and burnt herself!

N-ICE FLOOR, DAD

When the wooden floorboards in the dining room were looking worn from all the walking in and out of the kitchen, Derek decided to give that particular area a polish.

Getting down on hands and knees he polished the two foot patch by the kitchen door to a shiny gleam. Shiny and... slippery. After slipping several times carrying food from the kitchen, his wife told him never to do it again. But his kids enjoyed it. When they were in their socks, it made a great mini skating rink. So Derek has continued to polish it ever since!

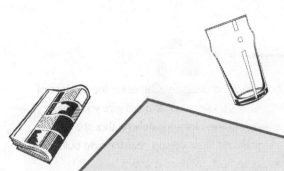

I have found the best way
to give advice to your children
is to find out what they want and
then advise them to do it.

**Former US President,
Harry S Truman.**

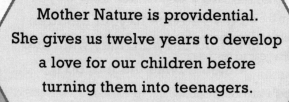

Mother Nature is providential.
She gives us twelve years to develop
a love for our children before
turning them into teenagers.

William Galvin

VACATION: IMPOSSIBLE

Shortly after the filming of *Mission: Impossible II*, Tom Cruise took a holiday with his kids while his then wife, Nicole Kidman, worked on *Moulin Rouge*.

He was all smiles as he boarded a 40-foot fishing boat with Connor, five, and Isabella, seven, but things were far from ship-shape. "We were like The Griswold family from *National Lampoon's Vacation*!" recalls Tom. A motor conked out, a jet ski ploughed into the side and the boat struck a reef. When the fire from the on-deck barbecue roared a little too high in Connor's direction, Tom shoved the grill overboard. He later donned scuba gear to rescue it!

Isabella later described the trip to her mum. "It was tragic," she declared. "Then fun!"

WHERE'S DADDY?

Lenny couldn't take his eyes off his little girl, Katie, as she smiled from ear to ear on the fairground carousel. Each time she went past him, he smiled and waved. Smiled and waved. Smiled and... then his friend came along. They got chatting and Lenny walked off with him, completely forgetting about Katie.

Thankfully he remembered before he had walked too far off. But he returned to a now crying and distraught little girl. Time for some candy floss, Dad!

HEALTHY HAMSTER

When composer Andre Previn and his wife applied to adopt
a Vietnamese orphan, a woman from the orphanage arrived
to stay with them for the weekend in order to assess their
suitability as parents.

At breakfast on the first morning, Andre poured her some
health food cereal and, keen to impress, talked about its
nutritional value and how much his sons enjoyed it. She sat
eating in silence before saying, "To be honest, I'm not crazy
about it."

Andre glanced at the grain-filled jar and replied, "I'm not
surprised. I've just made you eat a large bowl of hamster food."

YOU MEAN THEY EAT?

Colin was left at home looking after his 18-month-old son
when his wife went out. She was gone from ten in the morning
until four in the afternoon. She returned to find a bawling child.
"What did you give him for lunch?" she enquired. "Lunch?"
replied Colin. "Nobody mentioned lunch."

The young always have the same problem - how to rebel and conform at the same time. They have now solved this by defying their parents and copying one another.

Quentin Crisp

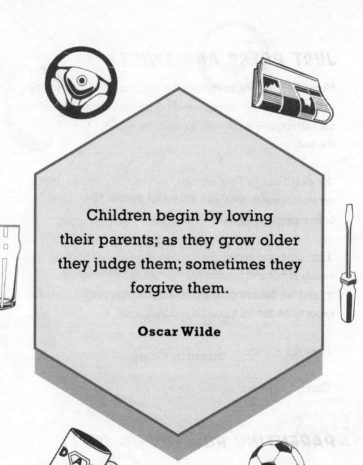

Children begin by loving
their parents; as they grow older
they judge them; sometimes they
forgive them.

Oscar Wilde

JUST PRESS AND TWIST

Mum was struggling to remove the 'child-proof' lid on a canister of tablets when her three-year-old daughter, Georgia strolled into the bathroom. "I know how to do it, Mummy," she said.

"It's okay, Georgia, I can manage," said mum. Georgia watched her continuing to struggle with the lid for a few moments before piping up again.

"I *can* do it, you know," she insisted. Mum stopped, smiled weakly at her and handed her the tablets so that she could try and fail. But to her astonishment, Georgia pressed down expertly on the lid, turned it and lifted it off.

"How did you know how to do that?" said mum.

"Daddy taught me," replied Georgia.

PARENTING HOLLYWOOD STYLE

When movie actor Adam Sandler was asked how he felt about becoming a father, he replied, "I'm nervous about it. I know when you have a baby it requires staying up all night and you have to rock them to sleep and change the diapers. And I don't know if my butler can handle all of that."

TRAIN TRAUMA

Whenever they went to London, Trish's dad thought it was great fun to get on an underground train with her and jump off, pretending to abandon her. He then jumped back on just before the door closed. Even now, at the age of 22, Trish hates travelling on the underground.

DRAMA QUEEN

A red-faced dad whose daughter was bitten by a deadly tiger snake, thought she was simply being a 'drama queen.'

Elizabeth, 12, was bitten while walking near the Werribee River in Melbourne, Australia, but managed to walk 500m back to her friend's house before succumbing to the poison. Elizabeth's parents took her to hospital but dad Ian thought the wound on her big toe looked more like a scratch than a bite.

"She said she saw a snake slithering away but Elizabeth is a bit of a drama queen so I had my doubts about it," he said. "I thought it was probably a lizard that scratched her but I took her to hospital anyway, just to be safe.

"When tests showed that it was the bite of a deadly tiger snake and that she could have died, I felt awful."

182

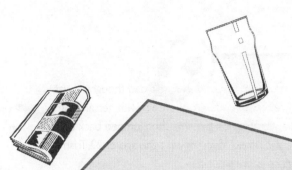

My dad always used to tell me that if anyone challenged you to an after-school fight, tell them that you won't wait. You'll kick their ass right now.

Cameron Diaz

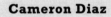

My father was frightened
of his mother. I was frightened
of my father and I am damned well
going to see to it that my children
are frightened of me.

King George V

PLANE CRAZY

Joker Brian put his toddler daughter Jessica on the luggage carousel at the airport. Just for a laugh, like you do. But he began to panic when he couldn't reach her because of all the people in the way. Seeing him looking worried, she began to scream and he just managed to rescue her in time before she disappeared behind the curtain.

FAMILY FEAST

As a treat for his kids, Jim said he would order a Chinese take-away for the family to enjoy. Leaving his wife to ask the excited youngsters what they wanted he returned to find that she had written the order on a piece of paper. Jim then telephoned the restaurant and started to give his order. "128 chow mein, 62 sweet and sour chicken, 57 prawn balls, 98... er... hang on a minute. That can't be right. It seems rather a lot for four people. Oh! I see. She's written down the dish numbers. Not the quantity. Er... can we start again?"

You don't want your kid
to be the carrot kid. There's always
the kid at the birthday parties
carrying a bag of carrots. You've
got to let them eat a little cake.

Tobey Maguire

DAD ATE FAMILY PETS

A drunken dad from Yorkshire broke his son's heart by eating his pet stick insects at an *I'm A Celebrity* theme party.

Adam, seven, had named his stick insects Matt, Charlie and James after his favourite pop band, Busted. But his dad, Pete, wolfed them down after organising his own Bush Tucker Trial.

Pete had invited five pals over to watch the *I'm a Celebrity... Get Me Out of Here!* final on TV. Getting into the spirit of things, they had their own version of the Bush Tucker Trial, eating fish eyes, tripe, ox tongue, raw eggs, tequila worms... and stick insects.

Adam burst into tears when he found out and wife Mandy kicked him out of the family home. The ashamed dad later said, "The tequila was flowing all night and we were so drunk that we would have eaten almost anything. I remember us arguing over who the winner was and someone said we could settle it by seeing who would be the first to eat a live insect.

"One of the lads spotted Adam's stick insects in their tank and said, 'What about one of those?' The others seemed to be dithering but I decided to go for it and wolfed all three down so there was no doubt about the winner. I really wish someone had stopped me.

"I felt awful in the morning when I realised what I had done. I've been an absolute idiot. I feel like the world's worst dad."

BABY? WHAT BABY?

A dad left his six-week-old daughter alone in his car for six hours to go boozing in a nightclub – then went home to bed without her.

He had so much to drink that he ended up getting a lift home and forgot all about tiny Lilly. Later, he was woken by his frantic wife, Kelly, at 5.30 am when she discovered that Lilly was missing from her cot.

At first he told his wife he had forgotten where he had parked his car with the baby inside and had lost his keys. Eventually, he remembered he had left it in a seafront car park opposite a nightclub.

Paramedics then rushed to the scene to find Lilly still inside in a carry cot. They had to break a window to get her out and take her to hospital for health checks.

Man, if I can get a burp out of that little thing I feel such a sense of accomplishment.

Brad Pitt

Prince William is wonderful. When I met him at the Queen's Jubilee Concert, I said "I have got a daughter for you."

Ozzy Osbourne

DOUBLE TROUBLE

Martin Davidson felt like the worst daddy in the world after he
unintentionally caused two major injuries to his four-year-old
daughter, Chloe, in two weeks.

When he accidentally shut the bathroom door on her hand,
it took off the tip of her finger. Martin's wife, Nicola, heard her
scream and, being an auxiliary nurse, knew what to do. She
wrapped her finger in ice and took her to hospital where it was
stitched together.

"But we didn't expect what happened next," says Nicola.
"Martin took her to the park and he rang me at work to tell me
she had fallen off the climbing frame. She had broken her leg
and had to spend another night in hospital. The doctors said she
should get a season ticket!"

I guess somewhere between
kid number one and number seven,
I must have learned a few things.

Mel Gibson